Reflections from a Former Evangelical

Poems Reminiscent of My 2019 Worldview*

Nicki Pappas

*subject to change as I do

To 19-year-old me.
There's still so much to learn.
That's more than okay, beloved.

Also by Nicki Pappas

As Familiar as Family: Leaving the Toxic Religion I Was Groomed For (2022)
*Reflections from a Former Evangelical: Poems Reminiscent of My 2019 Worldview** (2022)
Becoming Egalitarian: Our Journey from Hierarchy toward Mutuality (2023)
*More Reflections from a Former Evangelical: Poems Reminiscent of My 2020 Worldview** (2024)

Inside You Will Find

Part A.
Introduction

About This Collection of Reflections

Back when I first wrote the poems in this book, I shivered at the thought of releasing them into the world. Fearing further ostracism, my reservations were strong. Here's the thing: in my faith excursion, I had just recently exchanged core beliefs. And, get this, there was *more to explore*. Therefore, I also worried that the words I enclosed in this particular book would be irrelevant in the future because I realized even then that as a human, I am always processing new information and evolving. But I wanted to document where I was in those moments and where I have been. I deeply desired to hold out hope for others like me who were feeling like spiritual misfits as they broadened the narratives they were taught within white evangelicalism.

As I explain in the introductory poem that follows, I want to use my writing to address suffering and remind people of their dignity. In April 2019, I participated in National Poetry Writing Month for the first time. I joined the Fight Evil With Poetry Facebook group and attempted to write a poem each day corresponding to the prompts that were provided. When I opened this document again in September 2022, each poem underwent some editing. Some were subject to a heavier hand of revision than others. The poems in Part B are my responses to a prompt a day. Lighter prompts were requested in the group, and the poems I wrote for those prompts are in Part C. The prompts are included so you can write your own responses if you'd like.

The second half of this anthology contains more poetry, and all of my musings were written in 2019, unless otherwise indicated. Part D is a timeline that captures the beginning of my trip down the so-called "slippery slope," a term used to discourage people from letting curiosity be a guide in spiritual matters. The poems were not written in chronological order. After the writing process was complete, I rearranged them to flow sequentially. (It's worth noting that I'm still on the "slippery slope," which makes sense considering how steep the mountain of my perceived religious superiority was.) In Part E, the conclusion, I wrote two poems about discovery. The first is about rediscovering who I am. The second details my discovery of new depths of God on this journey.

After I completed this collection, I entered it into a few writing competitions. It never got picked up. I assumed that because my manuscript never "won," no one would want to read these poems. Maybe that's true, but after self-publishing my memoir *As Familiar as Family*, I was looking for a way to fuse some joy back into my writing. That's when I remembered these poems. The original writing process of these poems was cathartic and enchanting for me, and I wanted to tap into those feelings again by revisiting them. I desire for my healing to fuel your healing as we travel together toward dignity-enhancing theologies and ideologies. Also, references to patriarchy, infanticide based on external anatomy, sexual trauma and violence (including rape and pedophilia), racism, homophobia, and transphobia, language that may be offensive to some readers, suicidal ideation, and spiritual and psychological abuse are present in the experiences included in these pages. Thank you for holding space for me. As always, I'm sending so much love to you.

-Nicki

No Longer Confined

I'm warmly embracing
A universal approach
Leaving evangelical as a label
It's a loaded term
Splitting the seams of an ancient suitcase
The rusty latches locked long ago
To exclude anyone deemed unorthodox
By those who hold the keys

I'm wandering labelless in the wilderness
Some will probably label me a heretic
Or think I'm sporadically switching sides
It's embarrassing to think
I somehow knew more
Than my newfound guides
As if I had figured out the infinite
And Divine Mystery could be contained
By the frame I maintained

These are my thoughts at this time
They are subject to change as I do
I reserve the right to change my mind
I am ever evolving
If I waited until I was fully satisfied
And completely certain of each claim I've made
These poems would never see the light of day

I just want to create
Not for money and not for fame
But because all this suffering
Cannot be in vain
As I've wrestled through grief
And been ostracized for these beliefs

Even if in the future
I would say these things differently
I must write as I seek
To remind everyone of their dignity
Come with me into flourishing
Come live free

Part B.
A Prompt a Day

Wake Up
April 1ˢᵗ prompt: write a poem about a dream

When we wake up
Those with the power lament
"All hell has broken loose"
Never once considering that maybe
Just maybe
Heaven is breaking through

The sun wakes
Bronze hues bathing
Just demands for equality
The nightmare continues
With cries of (cishet) men having
God-ordained authority

In their dream world
They talk of head coverings and headship
Cranial capacity and head circumference
Beliefs that linger still
Confirming for them and their dreams
Their supposed superiority

These delusions of grandeur lead them
To devalue others' bodies and minds
Emotions and souls
As they buckle down on roles
And treat mutuality
As an attack on the gospel
Can we not?
That'd be great
Thanks

If you're complementarian
I want to say I may be wrong
But, honestly, so might you
In all I do
I want my neighbors
To know they are valued and loved
Entering humble dialogue

Could save the lives of people like me
Could lead to a world where

We wake up and the words
"It's a girl"
Will no longer kill us
Where our genitalia
Won't be a death sentence
And none of us are brought home alive
Just to die inside
Knowing our dads
Would have preferred boys
That's right
We didn't miss your fallen face
About the pink center of that cake

So, I will dream
I will aspire
I will live to lift us higher
While shaking awake the sleeping ones
Because there's work to be done

Moving from Heel to Hill to Heal
April 2nd prompt: write a love poem to your hometown

I grew up in "the church"
Spent my life on a search
For meaning and purpose
As I moved
From town to town to town
I was eighteen
When I struck out on my own
Entering the "big city" I felt at home
For the very first time
Became catechized
Was baptized
(For the second time)
Quoted verse by verse
(All the time)
I belonged
In Rock Hill

Only big from my point of view
When compared to Liberty Hill
The country community I left behind
That doesn't even have a traffic light
Moving confirmed my accent was thick
In Rock Heel

It was here an unstable foundation
Was built upon
Where I learned to spend hours
Poring over systematic theology
Telling myself that of course knowledge
Didn't save me
Week in and week out
Articulating the words of a gospel
I didn't know was truncated
Beating myself up
Putting myself down
Shame became the pool
Where I almost drowned
In Rock Hill

But a movement started
I became conscious
A couple years and Be the Bridge later
This is where I really learned
To love God and neighbor
By confronting the idol of white supremacy
To wrestle with doubt and uncertainty
Alongside others feeling the same as me
To seek justice
Love mercy
Walk humbly
In Rock Hill

Caring less of what people think of me
Breaking away from all toxicity
Embracing who I am in all my passion
To belly laugh again
In Rock Hill

Almost a decade and a half has passed
Since I unloaded my first box
It was here where I fell in love
With coffee and my partner
In that order
Traveled the five-year road
To graduate college first-gen
Home delivered three babies
Deconstructed and am reconstructing faith
Hoping against hope it isn't too late
Sorrow and bliss mixed
Creating a life full of living
As I heal
In Rock Hill

The Path to Power
April 3rd prompt: write a poem inspired by power

What is power?
Why do we want it?
The subtle allure
Of making the world perfect
Or at least better
But for who?
For you, of course, but also for me
Because it's just too exhausting
To be the change I want to see
Holding the power
Would make progress easy

The path to power is littered
With people who had the best intentions
Climbing the ladder
Of social and political capability
Promising to use their influence for good
Christians grasping for biblical proof
To advance their own agendas

Here's the thing
Jesus taught toward ending hierarchy
Yet some of these men have the audacity
To attack me in their fragility
With their toxic masculinity
Sexism
Patriarchy
And blatant misogyny
Feigning godly orthodoxy
Working out wicked orthopraxy
They question my motives
Suspicious as if I am suspect
After all, it was Eve who was deceived
And Mother Eve's deception
Became my perpetual perception
"Women, can't trust 'em
Because they trust their feelings"
Our intellect debated

We are relegated
To childbearing and barefoot cooking
Washing dishes in the kitchen sink

Christians, this is my plea to you
In the movements toward equality in our day
Cease with only listening to the people on your side
Please stop contributing to the divide
I ask you to no longer dehumanize
For then you cannot empathize
Be like the Jesus you say you love
Who came to upside-down empower
Showing that the path to power
Is only nobly traversed
By giving it away
To put the "last" first

Art in All Its Forms
April 4th prompt: write a poem about what art is or isn't

Move toward the discomfort
It will only last a little while
Or the duration of your entire life
Either way
It will be okay
Sit in any agitation
Even if it's not
Your initial inclination
There is so much beauty
On the other side

Sacred Body
April 5th prompt: write a poem about your body

Always too much
Never enough
All the standard clichés
Of not measuring up

Measuring waist size
Comments on my thighs
Hips good for childbearing
Change what you're wearing

Wearing me down
Critiques don't abate
The gaze of men
An unappeasable weight

The weight on the scale
A consuming score
I need to eat less
And exercise more

An exercise in self-love
Embracing this figure
I'm now proud of
With every flaw and curve

Flawed is no longer the lens
Used to view
This frame that is frail
Yet so powerful and renewed

Powerful enough to grow
And birth three babies
Stomach covered with
Marks that keep stretching

Stretched thin
Physique policed
Modesty mantras
That just don't cease

Cease the objectification
Stop with the tired conflations
Put away every accusation of making men trip
For this sacred body is a place of worship

[Note: Our bodies are powerful regardless of whether or not we conceive or give birth.]

A Revolution Inspired by Luther's "Reformation"
April 6th prompt: write a poem about either reformation or revolution

I don't have 95 theses
To put on a message board
But I am troubled by the clergy
While I urge repentance
Coupled with reparation(s)
It is past time for a reformation
Scratch that
There's no reforming this
It must be torn down and rebuilt

The Christian Church as an institution
Needs to give an account for their dilution
And intentional collusion with the empire
And for all that has transpired
To keep power in the hands of the mighty
No more excuses

There is more than enough
Theological scholarship
For you to be equipped
With an interpretation
That honors the people
You marginalized
Be a place of respite
From the categorization
Not the perpetuator or sustainer
If you want to join the mission of Jesus
Here's a revolution for you

Like Butterflies and Moths
April 7th prompt: write a poem about butterflies and moths

Butterflies and their cousins the moths
Lepidoptera insect family the same
Varied in more than just a name

Butterflies
Thin antennae with knobs at the end
Beauty I struggle to comprehend
Diurnal, gracing the skies during the day
Full-fledged glory on display
Wings behind when not on the move
Up to 20,000 species with nothing to prove

Moths
Antennae thicker and feathery
Every bit as lovely
Nocturnal, coming out at night
Crowding the front porch light
Opening their wings to rest
Before taking off on a quest
Most of the 160,000 species are dull in color
But catching a glimpse still fills me with wonder

Both holometabolous
Undergoing metamorphosis
Egg to caterpillar
Emerging adult from a chrysalis
The only insects with scales covering their wings
Forming patterns to keep from being seen
Camouflage protection
Resembling leaves and tree bark
To hide from predators like the owl and lark
Complete transformation
Making a great migration
Like the eastern population
Of the monarch butterfly

Fluttering
Flapping

Flitting
Blending in
Standing out
Nectar sipping
Lumped together
Separated into groups
Discovering exceptions
To the so-called rules

Actual Good News
April 8th prompt: write a poem about one of your favorite stories

One of my favorite stories ever told
I hope to be telling when I am
Gray, tired, forgetful, and old
Is one from which numerous stories unfold

It's a story of redemption
Of making new
Repairing all that is broken
That affects me and you
The story of someone who cared enough
To enter our suffering
Someone who listens to creation's groans
And responds in love

In the story
The ultimate display of love from "above"
Was fully present in and active through
The actions of the one called Jesus
The story goes that for about 33 years he lived
He resisted temptation again and again
The temptations of performance and possessions
Of power and popularity
Because he knew his identity
Was secure without these things

He taught and he healed
He broke bread and filled
Hungry stomachs
Removed physical barriers
Contextualized what he communicated
Saw and sat down
With those on whom the powerful frowned
Empowered women
Brought them in
As some of his closest disciples and friends

He explained the Scriptures saying,
"The Spirit of the Lord is upon me.

I was sent to proclaim liberty to all those in captivity,
To ensure none of the oppressed are left behind.
I was anointed to proclaim good news to the poor
To declare the year of the Lord's favor."

Jesus's mother Mary said,
"My spirit rejoices in God my Savior.
He scattered the proud and overturned power structures
By bringing the mighty beneath those who live humbly.
He filled the hungry with good things.
The rich he sent away empty."

For those with wealth and authority
I can understand why they would subvert
These upside-down messages
Make them spiritual rather than physical
The original ones who forsook the gospel
Now discrediting those pursuing something "social"

It's said that Jesus broke down
Dividing walls of hostility
Love causing us to discern our distinctions
Not ignore or delete them
Replacing condemnation
With affirmation and celebration

I was told that Jesus destroys
Even the most protected of idols
And requires us to not be idle
To repent whenever we are complicit
Rally together as a team of misfits
Not conforming to the ways of this world
Where control is used to intimidate and lord
Following the teachings of this Christ
Doers of good news all the days of our lives

[Note: I once heard someone preaching say that we shouldn't refer to the "gospel of
Jesus Christ" as a "story" because that language implies that it isn't true. I'm more
than okay with this language now.]

Three Decades as Shoes
April 9th prompt: write a poem about being an article of clothing
and the people who have worn you

I am a pair of shoes, and I know it
Because they come in twos, and I hate being alone
I accept this because there's nothing inherently
Wrong in being this article of clothing

The past three decades of people wearing me
Most only used me to get them where they wanted to go
Walking on me for their convenience
With no regard for my well-being
But only for how I made them look
And I accepted this
I so often mistook certain words and types of treatment
As valuing me for who I am, not just what I can give

I became tattered and torn
Battered and scorned
Most people just trading me out
When I no longer met their needs
And I accepted this because I didn't know my worth

Now new material has been infused
I've been given a second life
Another chance
So I am only going home with the people
Who won't take advantage of me being shoes
Who appreciate that the comfort I bring
The support I offer
The touch of glitter on the sides
These are gifts
I am asking myself, "Why does this person want to wear me?"
And acting accordingly
I accept this because the behavior of another
Toward what they put on
Exposes truth about the character of the wearer
Not the one being worn
I am traveling the world soothing hurting people's feet
Knowing the ones who will care for me
As a beloved pair of shoes

Inequality Persists
April 10th prompt: write a poem inspired by equality

As long as white people are more worried
About being called racist
Than healing to be actively anti-racist
There will be work to do

As long as men are more worried
About being called sexist
Than healing to actively value us
There will be work to do

As long as white nationalists are more worried
About being called xenophobic
Than healing to actively include
There will be work to do

As long as cishet people are more worried about
Being called out because of their phobias
Than healing to actively embody that love wins
There will be work to do

Inner work
Outer work
Inner
Outer
In and
Out

My Reservoir of Memories
April 11th prompt: write a poem about an unimportant memory

I keep diving into the reservoir
Sifting through for an unimportant one
But when I think, "This is it"
I remember what it has done
How I was shaped and changed
For better or worse
Because of the memory

There are certainly
Memories I want to forget
And ones that make me reminisce

Blocked out
Blacked out
Laughter inducing
Tear producing
Anger rising
Numbness
Every emotion in between

Possibly useless information tucked away
Facts and stats I rattle off when I want to seem brainy
The name of someone who has long forgotten me
Or who I've already met but they introduce themselves
Every single time

But who knows
Maybe I'm taking the easy way out
Not conjuring up
A memory deemed unimportant

You Know Who You Are
April 12th prompt: write a poem about someone you don't understand

How much time do you have?
I could write all day
I'm asking
Exasperated
"Why are you the way that you are?"
Like Michael Scott to Toby
But really, I do wonder

Eyes glaring
Finger pointing
As if I shouldn't question
Your anointing
Harsh accusations
Here you come
With explanations
For the massive damage done
Attempting to excuse
Inexcusable behavior
And when that doesn't work
You go on to use
Tactics to
Deny
Dismiss
Discredit
Diminish

You manipulate
Want me to ingratiate
Grovel at your feet
Silently accept
The way you treat me
Let you speak cruelly
With no accountability
And simply be thankful
That you are willing
To put this behind us
Free yourself from true repentance

To borrow words
From Cardi B
You had me
Thinking I'm flawed (and even crazy)
When you are the one
Who is inconsistently
Selectively
Applying theology

Your skill level
In gaslighting
Is frightening
Tendencies that are narcissistic
Can't be empathetic
Can you take the
Focus off yourself
For just one second?
Understand the situation
From my point of view
Understand how much I do
Love you

I know you've been hurt
But I refuse to maintain
The misguided belief
That hurt people
Hurt people
This assertion is a thief
Robbing you and others
Of experiencing the relief
That flows from humility
I want to credit
Lily Hope Lucario
For breaking down this barrier
Her clarity is helping mend me
She explains
There are many people
Traumatized and abused
Who have compassion
These survivors would never
Intentionally leave someone bruised
Make a victim

Physically
Emotionally
Mentally
Spiritually
Psychologically
Because they don't desire
Inflicting pain on another
There is no valid excuse
Hurting people
Is something you choose

I will never understand
Your lack of empathy
And sympathy
Your willful inability
To view me
Through a lens of dignity
You said to tell you
If I think you sinned
Again and again I did
Yet you say you did not

Refusing to repent
Refusing to repair
Your words
Heaping shame
Too heavy to bear
In your world
People are dispensable
Disposable
Replaceable
It is irresponsible
For you to be leading a church
But the majority give you a crutch
And we all suffer for it

I worry for you
Your family
The well-being
Of the local Body
As we let pride persist
In our midst

I think of the warning in Proverbs 29:1
How long before you are broken beyond healing
Leaving everyone else reeling
Cleaning debris from the avoidable wreck
Because you stiff-armed completing
A comprehensive ego check

You know who you are
Or maybe you don't
Lacking self-awareness
You probably wouldn't think
There's no way this poem is or isn't about me
That's what makes all of this so scary

All the Reasons

April 13th prompt: write a poem about the most important album in your life

Selecting an album and dubbing it
THE most important in my life
Seems impossible
Not because I'm a music aficionado
But precisely because I'm not
There are few that I listen to each song
Without skipping
But there is this one
The work of Micah Bournes
A Time Like This is the name

Maybe it's because of who shared it with me
(S/O to the one and only Ruth)
Maybe it's because it's one I play on repeat
Laced with hard to digest truth
Maybe it's because of my transformation
As it bulldozed the remains of a faulty foundation
Maybe it's because I needed to be
Equipped with the message
For a time like this
Or maybe it's a combination of these expressions

The day the link was sent
I wept and spent
Hours sitting in lament
Repenting where I needed to repent
Another friend texted
"Tell me this isn't hype music for racial justice.
And it's from a place of faith?!?! I'm done!"
It solidified these people as my people

The tracks acknowledge pain
Educate
Shed light
Don't sedate
Address despair
Never placate
Demand action

Advocate
Spark hope
Rehabilitate
And exude all the joy

Most highly recommended for all the reasons
The lyrics applicable in every season
While reaching for the day
When some of the lines no longer are

The Value of Therapy
April 14th prompt: write a poem inspired by therapy

Undervalued
Devalued
Dare I say despised

On the contrary
Necessary
Should be highly prized

Friendships
Hardships
Authentic community

Lives intertwined
No one left behind
Will you come with me?

Mental health
Emotional wealth
Whole human flourishing

People who care
Shoulders that bear
Every burden carrying

Waterfalls
Phone calls
A scheduled session

Consistent
Persistent
Intentional intercession

Expansive
Expensive
Too costly to ignore

Don't suppress
Decompress
Seek healing more

Chasing after
Deep laughter
No longer numb

Moving past cope
Brimming with hope
Comforter, come

Simple Lines
April 15th prompt: write a poem about, or inspired by, someone else's poem

I keep repeating the words
That struck the chords
Deep within my soul
Resonating
Reverberating
Filling in the holes

Is There Strength in Me?
April 16th prompt: write a poem about your greatest strength

Defending my greatest anything
Causes my face to flush
Heart rate to rush
I used to be so confident
I don't know if it's false humility
As some would have me believe
Or the erosion of my dignity
That keeps me from acknowledging
Anything great in me

But if pressed to choose
My greatest strength would have to be
My comprehensive memory

The picture I slid from the album
Out of the flimsy plastic protector
My biological name
Scrawled across the back
I was just a child
But this is one of the earliest memories
I tucked away
Along the way
I continued observing
Remembering the seemingly insignificant
Realizing nothing is insignificant
Piecing together puzzle pieces
Constructing an imperfect picture
Answering my own questions relentlessly
Never asking for permission
To unlock sequestered secrets
Until confirming his identity

I joke that I'm Nancy Drew
Stephen said, "She's got nothing on you"
Repeating conversations almost verbatim
Words from a podcast interview
Quickly flipping to the page
That contains a breakthrough

Easily memorizing street numbers and avenues
Always keeping receipts
Collecting potentially life-saving information
Notes scribbled
Notebooks filled
Dates stamped
Screenshots captured
Learned now instinctive behaviors
For my protection

As impressive as these skills are
I don't want to give the impression
That I can evoke everything
There is still plenty that falls through the cracks
And both stress and depression
Resulting in numbness to the point of memory loss
Have had their way with me
But I don't see this as weakness
Just a reality of my humanity
Unconscious repression is strength often overlooked

I know it's not the best
But it's mine
And each memory I do or don't fully recollect
Gives evidence of power within even me
Restoring once eroded dignity

Slippery Slope
April 17th prompt: write a poem about an important belief that has changed

The house of my beliefs is crumbling
Stephen said, "You're pulling the rug out from under me"
Will there be anything left
When I've pushed every boundary?

I strapped on the skis
Took off down the slippery slope
Which is a caution conveniently voiced
To prevent intense exploration
Of a less cruel terrain's interpretation
I once was so certain women could not be pastors
But the vast amount of scholarship
On this one topic
Made me rethink my confidence
In this (shouldn't be controversial) subject
Why did I ever think
God would give women the gift of teaching
And then require them to not use it
To build up the Body
As commanded in 1 Corinthians 12?

The conflation of terms leads to confusion
Constricting
Restricting those who yearn
To exercise their gifts
Elder/*Presbuteros*
Overseer/*Episkopos*
Shepherd/*Poimen*
Pastor by another name
An elder, an older person, needs to be able to teach
Anyone can possess this gift to reach others

Then there are those that grab the verse in 1 Timothy 2
Misunderstanding teaching and exercising authority
Authentein only one time used in what we call the Bible
Elsewhere this word has a violent connotation
So of course, Paul wouldn't want women to abuse
But notice he doesn't command the men to

Opponents say I ignore plain and simple biblical reading
They apply the same arguments
As those who tried (and try) to justify slavery
Because of the desire to reinforce hierarchy
How could I hinder a sibling
From ministering as gifted?
Why did I think I had the definitive theology?
Oh, to be characterized by more and more humility

Divine Mystery doesn't fear my questions
Doesn't run from my doubt
Is a steady presence on the descent
As I don't figure things out
Jacob wrestled with God
Which brought him closer
Will I receive a semblance of closure?

My Steady Bestie
April 18th prompt: write a poem about an important person

Important more than just to me
Completely content living in obscurity
Probably won't go down in history
As a well-known global figure

I've said it before
But I'll say it once more
Continually on my mind
This man is compassionate and kind
One of a kind
Patient and humble
Constant in the calm
As well as the rough and tumble

He makes me laugh
Drives me crazy
Because of him I have three babies
Reminds me not to take myself
So seriously
Loves sacrificially
Restores dignity
Nurtures spaces that promote equality
Cultivates and helps unleash the best in me

Is there when I bawl
For all the ugly crying
My steady bestie
Hunkering down for the long haul
Fulfilling my dreams big and small
Like when he bought all ten cute Target cups
To fill the cabinet up
And stocks up the fridge with Starbucks frappes
And brings home caramel macchiatos
Because he knows the way to my heart
Is through coffee

Or when he worked multiple jobs
So I could study and get a degree

And assisted me with lesson planning
Paper grading
Tutoring
And chaperoning
When it was my ambition to teach
Present for every speech
Supportive of conferences where I was asked to present
Didn't criticize or resent when I wanted to quit
Counting me more significant

Now that I've adjusted my aim again
He's nourishing the person I am within
Encouraging me to follow my passions
Wherever they may take us
Modeling well Ephesians 5:21
Understanding what it means to be one
Ready to answer anyone
Who asks why we break free
From anything that fosters toxicity
Whether people
Places
Or ideologies

Peacemaking
Peacekeeping
Peace is a top priority
Your Enneagram 9 to my Enneagram 3
Not threatened by how much I achieve
Fourteen years together
Each dragging day fleeting
Learning intermixed with ignorance
In and out of bliss
Relationship evolving as we individually change
And rearrange firmly and loosely held beliefs

Forgiving quickly
Being forgiven
Resisting giving and receiving forgiveness
A couple of walking, talking contradictions
Hoping we occasionally get things right
Overcoming the despised indoctrination
Of the past decade
Together

Ruminating on Relationships
April 19th prompt: write a poem about something you often neglect

Relaxed or rigid
(Ir)regular rhythms
In relationships
Can inadvertently
Breed adverse
Repercussions
Forgetting reasons
To reflect
Revise
Refine
Recognize
Remarkability
Endeavors required
Reach out
Write words
Of refreshment
Get refreshments
Make reservations
Road trip
Read poetry
Rub shoulders
Literally
And figuratively
Receive
Reciprocate
Respond
Initiate
In relationships
For rich results
And robust rewards

Hypothetical Situational Death
April 20th prompt: write a poem about something you would die for

I don't trust myself to
With a clear conscience say
I would die for anything
Because I just don't know
I spend so much time in the hypothetical
But that's not necessarily beneficial
What circumstances would prompt my death?
Could I do anything to prevent it?
Was there no other way than self-sacrifice?
Would I act right away
Or would I have to think twice?
Is cowardice the explanation
For my reservation, my hesitation?
Would it be valor or vengeance
To confront danger that surrounds?
Protection or a privilege
To plant my feet to stand my ground?
What would my death accomplish?

In an effort to respond to the prompt
I could compile a list of possibilities
At one point Jesus would've been at the top
But what does it even mean to die for Jesus
Then there's my partner
Our three kids
Prisoners' release
Justice
The vulnerable
Sacred beliefs

All of this sounds noble
But I cannot say with certainty
I would unequivocally choose death
It would depend on the situation
Until then, should it come to pass
A scenario that may or may not one day play itself out
I can live for the "fruit of the Spirit"
To take deep root in me
That I may react accordingly

An Ode to Argentinian Cuisine
April 21st prompt: write a poem about another culture's food

Argentina summer
All the sweet treats
Café con leche
Cakes filled with
Dulce de leche
Medialunas
Followed by savory empanadas
And several asado feasts

Sharing a bombilla
Sitting, sipping mate
Made from yerba leaves
Infinitely better
In the presence of
Beautiful people
Who didn't need
A team of missionaries
To host English clubs
As a gateway to sharing "the gospel"

The Reversal of a Tragedy
April 22nd prompt: write a poem about a tragedy you would change if you could

The eleventh of September
In the year 2001
Is when a tragedy occurred
That I wish could be undone
Not just because of the
Precious lives lost that day
But also for those who have since
Been put in harm's way
Soldiers and civilians in lethal wars overseas
And here people from the Middle East
Who are only viewed
Through the lens of stereotypes
They are labeled as terrorists
Hate crimes are committed
As fear is festered
By white nationalist rhetoric
The "Never Forget" slogan
An attempt to justify bigotry
When trying to rob
Rashida Tlaib and Ilhan Omar
Of their dignity
Brown skin is portrayed
As a threat to public safety
When what these political figures mean
Is a danger to the ideas
Of white and Christian supremacy
Islamophobia fueled
By misunderstandings and assumptions
Excuses for not building relationships
That disrupt presumptions

Power, Privilege, and Triggers
April 23rd prompt: write a poem inspired by trigger warning

Power alters
The brain's ability
For feeling empathy
Privilege affords power
And the other way around
Consequences scarcely found
More privilege requires less need
For receiving content/trigger warnings

The War Fought to Preserve Slavery
April 24th prompt: write a poem about a historical event
your perspective has shifted on

I believed for the longest time
The carefully curated lie
By sympathizers to the confederacy
That the Civil War was simply
A misunderstanding concerning states' rights
Ignoring the verifiable reality
Of their desire to defend
The idea of white supremacy

People like members of the UDC
The original writers of revisionist history
The Lost Cause myth sustained in textbooks
For generation after generation to overlook
Thinking it's okay to "own" a human is totally depraved
The immorality was more than understood by the enslaved

I bought into the narrative that assuages white guilt
And the delusion of the benevolent master
Not wanting to think this empire was built
On genocide
Brutality
Greed
Separating families
And degrading humanity

Information that is accurate is embarrassingly easy to access
If the Civil War was fought for states' rights in any capacity
It was for the "right" to preserve the disgusting ideology
That considered people property

Work in Progress
April 25th prompt: write a poem about your ideal epitaph

We didn't always agree
But she led with curiosity

Hypocritical Me

April 26th prompt: write a poem about something you consider evil

When a woman "caught in adultery"
Was brought to Jesus
His words and actions
Brought her freedom
Her accusers quoted
Moses' law
Jesus protected her
Despite her assumed flaws
"Let he who is without sin
Cast the first stone"
We're told the only one who could have
Is Jesus alone
But rather than hurl a rock
He covered her with mercy
There was no condemnation
Oh, the scandalous controversy
If I were the woman
I would want to experience grace
But since I'm convinced I'm not
I study theology and place
Burdens on people
That are too much to bear
All the while
Pride puffs me up like a hot air balloon
Preventing the ability for me to perceive
The biggest hypocrite in the room

[Note: In 2019, I interchanged hypocrite and Pharisee. In 2021, I read tweets from people who are Jewish telling Christians not to do this, so I stopped.]

Nicki with a C-K-I
April 27th prompt: write a poem about your middle name

I go by Nicki
People then ask, "Is it N-I-K-K-I
N-I-C-K-I
Or does it end with a Y?"

On the first day of school
During the dreaded roll call
I just wanted to crawl under the desks
Rather than going through the whole spiel
That catches some serious side eye from all who hear it
Who probably doubt if what I'm saying is even real
Or who cringe as I awkwardly stumble along
The verbal path of my name origin story
Always offering up too many
Unnecessary, unasked for details
Because this is just who I am
Even to the attendant at graduation
Or in the waiting room for an appointment
Or to the friend I wrote a check to for reimbursement
Who didn't know that she shouldn't inquire
Most get an uncomfortable look on their face
As eyebrows raise while they say my first name
Rarely is it pronounced right the first time
Usually it rhymes with onion
This is followed by my clarification
"It's Minyon, like filet mignon"
Which launches me into the lengthy
Oral history of how this came to be

"Mignon means cute in French
Do you agree?
But spelled differently
Add a y and subtract the g…
No, that's not why she chose it
She stole it from a friend who liked it
And my middle name is Nicole
All of this doesn't really matter though
Because I go by Nicki with a C-K-I"

Beliefs that Ostracize
April 28th prompt: write a poem about being an outsider, using animal imagery

I feel like a discarded dog
Wandering the streets
Searching for people
Who won't ostracize me for my beliefs

Begging at the fence
Digging a tunnel to get inside
Because I desperately want
Acceptance on the other side

Hear me out
Hear me howl
The threat of excommunication
Tempts me to bow

If these are positions
I'm too afraid to publicly own
Should I even hold them
While looking for a home

But I can't, no I won't
Prostrate myself for a treat
Pledge my unfailing allegiance
At their idol's feet

I'm refusing to yield to those
Who try intimidating with power
I will bare my teeth
And I will not cower

To the Religious Bent on Dispensing Retributive Punishment
April 29th prompt: write a poem inspired by prison

Cease with praying, "Your Kingdom come"
If you want to keep locking people up
Unless you think there are cages in the "hereafter"
They have no place here

The physical chains you escaped
When you premeditatively raped
Or when you fed your pornographic wishes
With neighborhood kids
Or when you broke the speed limit
Weaving in and out of traffic
Continually getting away
With putting others in danger
Selfishly seeking to satisfy yourself
At the expense of everyone else
But you think possession of marijuana
And other nonviolent crimes
Should rob people of years living life

Even when they've paid their dues
You think all they should be allowed to do
Until the end of their days is suffer
Because their past choices should've been better
As if you always only choose to act wisely
And don't even get me started on the 94% plea deals

You say you've been shown great mercy
But if you really believed this
In the deepest corridors of your heart
You would show great mercy

You are bent on dispensing punishment that is retributive
Consider the difference if we practice justice that is restorative
Imagine a system that rehabilitates
Where we walk alongside one another and celebrate
Accomplishments, achievements, and victories
Ushering in true peace and thriving dignity

A Rolodex of Recollections
April 30th prompt: write a poem about the most fun you've ever had

The most fun I ever have
Is when I'm with friends
Who will do the unexpected

Approaching strangers to inquire
"Do you want to do the chicken dance?"
Clap-clap-clap-clap

Belting out songs from animated greeting cards
Nodding to unsuspecting customers
"Happy birthdaaaaayyyyy to youuuuuu"

Following a local celebrity home
(Not stalking because then we sound creepy)
"That's him! Quick, change lanes"

Interacting with the waiter
Only using words from Candy Crush
"Delicious"

Deciding that life is a Broadway musical
Singing into the void of night
"Just you and I, defying gravity"

Struggling into a full snowman suit
And strutting down the center aisle
"Work it, work it"

Laughter is healing medicine
For this weary, wounded soul
Finding joy in the everyday
Making merriment in the mundane
Pursuing pleasure in the pain
To create memories that cause
My heavy heart to hope
My fallen face to float
As I dare to embody delight

Part C.
These Were Supposed to
be on the Lighter Side –
Not All of Them Are

It All Started with a Trastle
prompt: write a poem that mashes two words together
written: May 7th

Right after the rush of breakfast
But before the real busyness begins
There's a general calm
As much as there can be
With three small children
A sort of stillness
As I sip my coffee on the couch
Sit in the joy
Soak in the ordinary
My girl
Creatively constructing
A truck castle
AKA a trastle
The wonder
Of devising and designing
With Duplo blocks
Engineering stability
Before demolishing

These are the moments
That are few and far between
When the Earth's spinning seems a little slower
When I see kindness winning a little more
Because within the half hour
The hollering and hoarding
Of all the toys will commence
Diapers that need to be changed
Dirty underwear thrown away
Due to the third accident this week
Until then, I smile while they take turns crawling in my lap
Maneuvering the cup of lukewarm motivation
To my lips
Around tiny shoulders
Annoyance and immense appreciation oscillating
Catching my breath
Because it won't be long
These days and trastles will soon be gone

Tokenized Woman

prompt: write a poem inspired by or in the form of a limerick
written: May 13th

There once was a woman tokenized
Her words elevated and justified
Misogyny, calling for
Fuel to continue war
Marking all who disagreed as despised

Meeting My Crush
prompt: write a poem about an embarrassing moment you laugh at
written: May 13th

I'm not sure how
So many people knew
About my celebrity crush
From the local news
But when I attended an event
And he was there, too
My friend's dad said
"I have someone to introduce you to"
Stephen with me
His wife by his side
I simply said, "Hello"
I had no reason to hide
Until the dad asked me
"Are you in heaven right now?"
I still can't believe
That's how it went down
I couldn't even smile then
My cheeks had a noticeable blush
Soon I could laugh but learned to
Conceal the name of any future crush

Say Hey Guys
prompt: write a poem about an inside joke
written: May 13th

She was out of town
He was moping around
We decided to spend some time with him
The chances of not cheering him up were slim
Because epic occurrences abound in the presence of
The Pappases?
The Pappi?
Let's just go with Big Steve and I

When she called to check in
He pretended to be sad
His voice full of sorrow
She was clearly irritated
Since she'd be home like tomorrow
So he told her he was just kidding
And that we had come over
He pointed the phone in our direction
And gave the simple direction
For us to say hello
He didn't know the plan we were brewing

I still laugh uncontrollably
When I think of how we locked eyes suddenly
Nodded our heads in agreement
And just sat silently
He had no idea what we were doing
"Say hey guys. Guys, say hey"
His voice now filled with urgency
As we ran and hid in the pantry
Before he could snap a picture
As proof of our company

He got real tired of this anecdote
But it will always be one of my favorite inside jokes

The Power of Narrative(s)
prompt: write a poem about an animated character
written: May 16th

I have an issue with historical fiction
That's geared toward kids
Perpetuating white savior propaganda

Empty Tomb. Also Cadbury Eggs.
prompt: write a poem inspired by whimsy
written: May 17th

I saw a social media post
"Happy Easter, you guys!!
He is risen!!
#ChurchAndWhimsy
#DontMakeMeChoose
#EmptyTomb
#AlsoCadburyEggs
He is risen!
He is risen indeed!"

The hashtag that got me
Was #DontMakeMeChoose
Juxtaposing church and whimsy
Cadbury eggs and the empty tomb
Because unfortunately some view the two
As diametrically opposed
And attempt to burden others with the belief
That celebrating the resurrection
Can't be paired with chocolate confections

Silly or serious are presented
As the only options
Not both
They say that would be contradictory
That there's the sacred or secular
Well, I think this is a false dichotomy
It's not either/or
There is no competition
We can cease with the asceticism
I'm convinced that Jesus
Isn't even a little worried

Not All Laughter Is Equal
prompt: write a poem about laughing
written: May 19th

I love to laugh
But IMHO
Not all laughter is equal

Prolonged or short bursts
Rising from the belly
Knee slapping
Breath gasping
Side holding
Church giggles that never end
Cycling over and over again

Through tears
Overflowing abundance
Brimming
Leaking from my eyes

Through cheers
Catching hold of every surprise
Twinkling
Twirling
Chasing fireflies

Through fears
That (sometimes) disappear
When a friend sits by my side
Hears my cries
Bears chocolate and wine
Or coffee and waffle fries
Healing catalyzed
Helps me compartmentalize
Reminds me of that one time

My most treasured though
Sacred and radical
Life-giving and empowering
Complex

Not making much sense
From a limited perspective
Is laughter as resistance
Joy displayed on someone's face
In the face of opposition
Clothed in strength and dignity
Head thrown back at the time to come
Taking a firm position
Laughing anyway

Part D.
A Timeline Not Written in Chronological Order

Racist Policies Built a Society That Continues Benefiting White People
written: Aug. 9th

Let's dig a little deeper
Trace it back
To the days of slavery and policies
Like the Homestead Act

People captured and sold
Based on the color of their skin
Oppressed and enslaved for the benefit
Of those with less melanin

The Indian Removal Act of 1830
Forced eastern Indigenous groups
Such as Creeks and Cherokee
West of the Mississippi

Colonizers moved to work the land
The government gave away acres
270 million
The Homestead Act disproportionately benefited white men
As Black people suffered by the law's implementation

There was insufficient follow through
On Sherman's promised 40 acres and a mule
Descendants of the formerly enslaved
Still need to be paid

Wealth accumulation secured a head start
Accompanied by segregated
Neighborhoods, schools, and jobs
Racist laws instituted and maintained
Drew red lines in the so-called United States

The Social Security Act of 1935
Ensured income to help the retired survive
But this safety net was not intended to catch everyone
The exclusion of agricultural workers and domestic servants
Meant many who were Asian, Mexican, and African American
Would not reap any of the benefits

Also passed in 1935
The Wagner Act inaugurated the right
For millions of workers who were white
To enter the middle class
While permitting the barring
Of everyone who wasn't white
From unions that could also deny
Hiring them for jobs with higher pay
And benefits including job security

As part of a New Deal program
The Federal Housing Administration
Along with the G.I. Bill
Allowed for Jim Crow accommodation
Resulting in decades of discrimination
Average white citizens and white veterans benefited
As the system was rigged for their advantage
Owning homes for the first time
While mortgage eligibility was overtly tied
To one's race

Segregation then and now is no accident
The government guaranteed the ways money was spent
Resulting in white families who would benefit
From secure financial stability for decades to come
While even in recent years Black and Latinx applicants
Are less likely to be approved for a loan
And white flight continues to persist

People who ardently insist
Racism is not systemic today
Wouldn't have recognized it
Any other day
Or they would have
But would continue to reject it
Because accepting the truth would require
Repairing the damage done by
White supremacy's layered lies

The Night That Started the Downward Spiral
written: Feb. 23, 2018

By the nightlight I sit here to write
As I lay awake, I could not sleep
As I replayed the events of the night
At that meeting
We agreed to stand in solidarity
But I am now weeping as I fear
I am not as valued by you
As I dared to believe
I spoke up and you remained silent
Rather than defending my honor
And calling another man to honor me, too
You sat speechless
Allowing him to ignore my leadership
And cause damage to me
And others
Not one of you men
Valued me enough
To beckon another man
To show me the same respect
Men receive
Am I not equal
In worth and dignity?
Am I this side of eternity
To be relegated to the status
Of a second-class citizen in the church?
I feel faint
What if all this waiting
Waiting for equality
Waiting for elevation to the
Same status as you all
Amounts to nothing
In the life hereafter?
(Is there life hereafter?)
Is misogyny my fate forever?
I fear it is
Fear envelopes
Fear is winning

Reparations before Reconciliation
written: June 21st

Christian, why are you against reparations?
I don't understand the disconnect
Between your orthodoxy and orthopraxy
Minds much more brilliant than mine
Have extensively covered this topic

Listen to the *Truth's Table* series "Reparations NOW"
Episode one roots this discussion in the gospel
Participating in righting the wrongs around us
Provides an opportunity to be obedient
To repair and repent
Episode two features Dr. Ana Lucia Araujo
Delivering global and historical receipts
Episode three is U.S. economic receipts
With Dr. Sandy Darity
Episode four covers ecclesiastical reparations
With Rev. Duke Kwon
I urge you to not move on in this conversation
Without learning from every one of these people

Read the work of Ta-Nehisi Coates
"A Case for Reparations"
If the recorded experiences
Don't cause you to feel angry
About the injustices in the housing market
I'm not sure we read the same piece

The final formative work I would recommend
Is *The Color of Compromise*
Jemar Tisby explains in chapter eleven
Reparations white Christians
Could easily implement
To institute and contribute
To a debt forgiveness plan for Black families
To establish trust funds for Black youth
To fund church plants and nonprofits led by Black people
To partner as churches and schools
To ensure Black students can attend without having

To pay tuition to colleges and grad schools
To financially support local public institutes
To guarantee Black students have what they need
To be educated effectively

If you want to push back by pridefully
Disagreeing with me
Arguing unproductively
Or defending your pursuit of "liberty"
While your neighbors suffer
I have neither the time nor the desire

Emulate Jesus
The one you say gave everything up
The one you say laid everything down
To love and serve the people around him

No more excuses
Open your wallet
Unclench your fists
And be generous

God of Second Chances
written: May 21st

I was told that you are a God of second chances
But I'm realizing more and more that your people are not
Unless someone like Trump or Kavanaugh is caught

Abundant Life Is Incompatible with Complementarian Theology
written: May 21ˢᵗ

An overemphasis on Ephesians 5:22
To the neglect of Ephesians 5:21
Means suffering for everyone

If we are expected to submit to men
Forfeit our voice
Left with no choice
Except in the narrow exception
Of if they ask us to sin
Then this is intruding on our calling
To exercise dominion
No wonder the fruit
Of complementarian theology
Is rotten and death inducing
As it's producing prideful narcissists
Who simply can't resist
Ruling over us

The depression
Suppression
Suspicion
The bruised bodies
Broken bones
And black eyes
Are no surprise

What does it mean for a husband
To love his wife as Christ
Unless you think Jesus expects us to
"Go to another place"
While he uses us for selfish purposes
Then a husband has no right to
Expect his wife to
Please him sexually
When she doesn't desire to
She shouldn't have to
Go somewhere else mentally

She should
And she does
Have the right to simply say, "No"

Further
It's incompatible to say
Christ came so we might have
Abundant life
Then to say
It's just part of living under the curse
That men would have to
Shoulder a heavy burden
All their days in leading
And the rest of us just have to
Live burdened
Thinking the worst
Wary of ourselves

Maybe many Christian men
Struggle with passivity
Because they were never meant to be
The only ones to lead
The very reason
People in Genesis were created
Was for it to be demonstrated
That humanity is to exercise stewardship
Together

An overemphasis on Ephesians 5:22
To the neglect of Ephesians 5:21
Means suffering for everyone

1 Timothy Can't Cancel 1 Corinthians
written: May 17th

How do I know
That in 1 Timothy 2 and 3
Paul didn't mean
People who look like me
Can't preach?

Because of 1 Corinthians 12

Not Trusting Women
written: May 21st

If you think women can't be trusted
To not be deceived
And they cannot lead
Or that if they do take control
And even do a better job than any man
God is displeased with them
For "not acting like women"
Can I have a word with you?

On the off chance you believe
God was working
In and through a woman
She is made the rare exception
To your arbitrary rule
While you lament what you perceive
As a shortcoming of men
To step up
So a woman
Can stay down

Do you think men have always
Wielded their weight wisely and well?
If men have been in positions of authority
For most of history
The war ridden relations of the past
And predicaments that plague us today
Are more likely connected to
The failure of men
Who fought and sought to secure
Privilege
Possessions
Popularity
Power

Do not dehumanize women
By trying to revoke our dominion
You cannot hide behind excuses
For why you do not trust us

Despised Indoctrination
written: May 18th

I despise the indoctrination
Of the past three decades

Despite the best of intentions
Rotten theology bears rotten fruit

A hardened heart, engulfing pride, and eroded dignity
Were the end results I'm still recovering from

Philip's Four Unmarried Daughters and My Single Sisters
written: July 5th

In Acts 21:9
Luke recorded a line
About Philip's four unmarried daughters
Who prophesied
Experiencing continued fulfillment of
The promise of Joel 2:28
God's Spirit being poured out on all humanity
As daughters joined in sharing prophecies

I have the great joy and privilege
Of knowing some unmarried women
My single sisters, I'm grateful for you
You each are vital parts of the Body
You love in ways that are unparalleled
When you exercise your gifts, my heart swells
The wisdom you so easily drop
Makes me want to stop
Everything I am doing
So I can soak in your every word
I don't want to miss any insight
Instruction, encouragement, rebuke

Some may say they don't know why
Luke wrote that the daughters who prophesied
Were unmarried
It doesn't take a seminary degree to know one's life station
Could bar from or open up opportunities
The writer wanted to demonstrate
That each member operates
From the status of a full child of God
There are no second-class citizens
Take notice Church

Sisters, you've made me better
I wouldn't be who I am today
Without your vulnerability
Thank you for trusting me
And for saying hard things

My Friend Invited Me into Freedom
written: May 14th

My dear friend was a rock
She facilitated healing in the aftershock
We praised God our lives were interlocked

She inspired
Pulled me from the mire
Sought to raise others higher

She invited me to be free
Helped me restore my dignity
Led the way to whole human flourishing

Calling In Is Not Divisive
written: Jan. 9th

Let's quit acting like calling in
Is inevitably divisive
If that were the case
Jesus created conflict
Each time he confronted people

Let's also not act like
It sows division
When someone seeks
To sew us together
By addressing harm publicly
This exposes pre-existing division
It is not preventing us
From living in unison

Let's also remember Jesus said
He came not to bring peace
But to bring a sword
Because hard truths uncover discord
Peeling back the layers of deception
Revealing the areas
Where we hold onto control
To the detriment of others
We're told Jesus achieved harmony
So we should be eager to receive
Inner and outer tranquility
By lovingly challenging one another
To pursue more than mere cordiality

But when authority is at play
We act like any talk that isn't directed
To the specific person is gossip
Which unsurprisingly silences victims
For so long those teaching the Bible
Have held the power
And for fear of losing their influence
They have interpreted it in a way
That stifles dissent

By making it seem like unveiling harm
Guarantees you're in violation of Matthew 18

I'm not saying that some who have suffered
Won't understandably experience bitterness
However, the possibility of resentment
Shouldn't prevent us from calling in
Leaders who are guilty of exploitation

Shame, My Only Constant Companion
written: May 30th

Shame
An all too familiar companion
Life is exhausting
When people pleasing
Drives decision making
Afraid of disappointing
Will I mess up again
Will I offend
Lose another friend
Did I fall too far this time
Past forgiveness that can
No longer be extended
Even though I am asking
Begging
Owning where I erred
This friendship
More fragile
Than I was prepared
Replaying
Reliving the scene
Wishing
I had done
Or said
Things differently

Shame
Is all I knew
Didn't know I needed
To grasp for freedom
Confined
In my mind
Defined by
Believing I am
What I did
Attracting
Being attracted to
Predatory people
Naively

Navigating narcissists
Thinking I can fix
All that is wrong
While they manipulate
To prove
I am worthy of love
From someone like that

Shame
Is closing in
As I just can't end
The cycle
The seven-time statistic
Returning to abuse
I'm so used
To being used
So I subject myself to
Whatever you want me to do
Because you won me back
I just don't know
It's temporary
As I desperately
Think that this time
Things will go differently

Shame
Is making me feel
That because I did
What is best for me
I am somehow
Failing people
Who didn't really give
A damn about me
Enlisting
New manipulators
To do their dirty work
In their social media feeds

Shame
Is not welcome here
Guardrails
And partitions

Put in place
To protect
The sacred space
Of my mind

Shame
Is a fog
Slowly lifting
One day at a time

Restored Dignity
written: May 21st

Nauseated at the thought
Of walking through those doors
And running into him
And no one who could
Do anything about it
Cared enough
To do anything about it

Realizing how little I matter
Made me wonder
What's the matter with me
I didn't know about my eroded dignity
Always walking out those doors
Feeling heavy

Until I accepted the invitation
Into healing and wholeness
Receiving me with open arms
Walking through those doors
Running into a warm embrace

Showing up
Showing out
Won't God do it
Feeling light as God puts up a fight
To rescue me from dangerous
Dignity robbing theology
I am worthy of every good thing

Burdens lifted
Experiencing God as a loving parent
Learning who God says I am
Known and pursued
Revealing the key
To restored dignity
That was in me
All along

Staying the Course
written: May 15th

"Staying the course"
This is a phrase used
As a goal is pursued
Regardless of criticism or obstacles

You wear the trauma like a badge of honor
As if God rewards those who willingly
Place themselves under oppression
While heaping condemnation
On those who choose not to

And according to you
Compared to me
It would seem you could bear more
Forgive and work through more
But no
I refuse to enable the harms
Inflicted by another
And call it Christian compassion
Toward this particular "brother"

You want the benefit of the doubt
While withholding the same from me
Grace cannot be given without
Telling truths that set us free

Staying the course for you
May mean staying put
But don't judge the limits of others
And the liberty they have
To experience healing elsewhere

Staying the course for me
Included putting
My foot down
Then bounding after joy
Into flourishing

Just because my faith
Is now lived out differently
Doesn't mean I have forsaken God
I wouldn't ever say that to you
So I don't understand the level of comfort
To direct this caution at me

Why are you expending energy arguing
Assigning the label of SJW to malign
When Jesus told his disciples
Everyone will know you follow me
Because of your love

The course of love
Is the one I want to stay on

Prioritizing the Privileged
written: May 7th

I've often wondered in recent days
What God thinks of the Christian Church
In the United States
That peddles a prosperity gospel
Saturated with the idea of white supremacy
Because of the conflation of Christianity
With white culture and identity
Which created a religion Jesus wouldn't recognize
Where the privileged are prioritized

We often prioritize the privileged
As evidenced by our
Prayers, politics, theologies
And tithings that center them

There was a parable Jesus taught
"Whatever you did
For the least of these
You did for me
And whatever you did not do
For the least of these
You did not do for me"

He didn't put any qualifiers
On the instructions
It doesn't seem to matter
If people are in specific situations
Because of "poor personal decisions" or not

Often, I think the line of needing to "be wise"
Is an excuse to hide behind a bias
And be able to clench our fists
Without feeling guilty about it

Read the warning in Matthew 25:41-46
Don't spiritualize the message of Jesus
May these verses be a catalyst
To quit prioritizing the privileged

Just Jesus
written: July 16th

"Just Jesus
As the focus"
The naysayers say
"Gospel-centered
[read Gospel-only]
Is the way things should stay
Otherwise, you are in danger
Of going astray"

"Injustice in us?
Certainly not"
And if I think so
There are consequences
If I choose to confront
Indeed, even insinuating
Needed change
Is a serious affront
"Intentions matter more
Not that impact doesn't matter
But you know we are good people
So this conversation doesn't matter"

Some desire agreeing to disagree
Which is not an option for me
When dealing with the ideas of
White, male, cishet, or Christian superiority
Others take a harsher approach
Their privileged lives threatened
They resort to threatening
To expose me and my "liberal agenda"
As if these threats should result
In me silently cowering at their feet
Pleading for them to keep
The lid on my dirty little secret
Oops looks like I beat you to it
The antitheses of Pandora's box
Has been opened wide in my life
Releasing antidotes

No injustice
In Jesus
We're told
Just words and actions
Healing
Hoping
Honoring
Forgiving
Feeding
Freeing
Resistance to unjust laws and customs
In his day

The life of this Jesus
One of
Restoring
Reconciling
Repairing
All things
Calling and equipping others
To do the same

A Jesus of justice
Is the focus
Righteous
Honorable
Just Jesus

What I've Been Accused of Now
written: May 21st

He just wanted to make sure
To lovingly caution us
That in all this talk of social justice
We weren't forsaking the gospel

It didn't matter that
In each referenced time together
We painstakingly connected
Civil rights and the good news

Never once
Before this period in my life
Did anyone accuse me
Of forsaking the gospel

I could read all the books
About being a "biblical" woman
That center on being a wife and mother
Spend hours discussing
Certain theological interpretations
While considering those doctrinal points absolute truth
Be completely consumed
With a more "spiritually acceptable" topic
And I guarantee he wouldn't accuse me
Of forsaking the gospel

She just wanted to make sure
To lovingly caution me
That in all this talk of mutuality
I wasn't finding my identity
In egalitarian theology

I was caught off guard and feeling weak
There is much I didn't speak
I'm not sure how helpful continuing
This conversation would ever be
But following each of her quotes
Is a glimpse into me

"I have the gift of discerning between the spirits"
Pulling out the spiritual gift makes it harder to push back
I have the gift of discernment, too
So was God communicating through me or you

"Every conversation this past year has circled back to gender"
I just started studying this seven months ago, so…

"What I saw was division"
Discomfort and tension
Reveal there is separation
Basically everywhere Jesus went
People got upset with him
He told us he came to bring a sword to divide
The mighty from those they marginalized
I perceive the truth as a medic
With high operating precision
To diagnose the problem
And make an appropriate incision
Removing toxic and suffocating ideology
Replacing it with beliefs that help us breathe
It is false unity if I simply sat silently
Concealing my anger is not indicative
Of living in harmony

"The old Nicki"
I can understand from your point of view
It looks like I have changed
This work transforms people
Making them able to feel more deeply
Hurt with those who are suffering
Who are silenced or dismissed
So we can
In the words of Mekdes Haddis
"Unmute the mic"

My friend had the opportunity to reach out
But I initiated the initial dialogue
I do regret not coming in more humbly
I owned where I erred
Asked for forgiveness
Not once but twice

But rather than showing me mercy
Or asking if I could help her
Understand my pain
She heaped on shame
Made me feel like shit
For disagreeing and expressing differing creeds
Her husband walked right past me
Not once but thrice
And did not once look me in the eyes
Or even acknowledge my presence
I cannot come to her with my deepest wounds
She demonstrated I can't
When she called what I did
The work of the enemy
I guess she doesn't perceive
She is just as susceptible
To deception as me

I could spout complementarian theology all day
And I did for a full decade
And never be accused by her
Of finding my identity
In complementarian theology

Being accused by even those
I thought were allies
I don't know why I was surprised
It has always upset those whose
Power and privilege are highly prized
When people intentionally
Value those the powerful marginalized
Point to the dignity of the socially despised
Amplify the voices of the disenfranchised
Emulating Jesus giving hope to the demoralized
The Jesus who saw through the disguise
And discerned those things that were idolized
How dare I care for Black lives?
Why should the stewardship of women be emphasized?

They think my views have polarized
I'm not even recognized
And I know this poem

May sound like I am upset
But this is just part of
My thought process
I took the time to pray
Wanting to fairly weigh
What she had to say
I approached and talked
With people I trust
Open to knowing if there were
Areas I needed to adjust
My hope is I will continue
To have a soft heart
But right now
Some temporary time apart
Seems to be the best solution
As I am on this journey
Toward a heavenly revolution

Alienation
written: May 21st

I did more than dip my toes in
At the very least I'm knee-deep wading
People seem concerned
As I am evolving and changing
Beliefs that were once core
Have shifted
Or altogether disappeared
And I have honestly never been better
I'm restoring my dignity
But I can't prove that to you
Our interactions characterized now
By your cautions and pity
With your hypocritical inconsistency
You alienate people like me
I want to offer reassurance
About my well-being
But *I* know I am being healed
And somehow that's enough
To abandon all this people-pleasing stuff

Yes, I'm Angry
written: May 27th

They ask, "Why are you so angry?"
And I wonder, "Why aren't you?"
Surely after everything we've been through
The least you could do
Is engage in basic elements of empathy
And simply sit with me

Yes, I'm sometimes angry
And there is nothing wrong with this
Anger can be a gauge
Indicating the presence of injustice
After everything that went down
"I gotta get outta this town"
Is certainly a thought that crosses my mind
Moving is an appealing option
I inhale and exhale a few deep breaths
I put some boundaries in place
Because instead of a new zip code
I just need some space

Anger isn't where I live
And when I am angry
It doesn't automatically mean
I have failed to forgive
I am learning to soak in every emotion
Even the ones I've feared
Hoping it inspires others like me
To be more human themselves

But First (and Second) Coffee Kind of Day
written: May 23rd

It's a "but first (and second) coffee" kind of day
Everyone is coming my way
I'm feeling need-to-lie-down tired
Too much is being required
So, I brew the grounds
While mounting pressures
Are brewing inside of me
Lifting my morning
And afternoon cups
Brings a little tranquility
Mugs with puns
Llamas
Unicorns
Gold lettering
Reminders of friends
Who love me deeply
I can't help but smile
Even if for just a little while

Hectic, Disconnected Life
written: Aug. 9th

Is this journey worth sacrificing certainty?
I will admit I enjoy this version of me
But I still struggle with people-pleasing

Life is hectic
I feel disconnected
From all I once knew
This time last year
I just wanted it all to be through
I was ready to meet Jesus face to face
If that's what even happens at the end
But Jesus met me in unexpected ways

Through a podcast here
A conversation there
A brand-new book
Every strained prayer
And even a sermon or two
My hope was slowly being renewed

There are literally loose ends everywhere
From my blanket of beliefs unraveling
It's true what they say about pulling one string
You just might undo everything
Left with fabric that no stitch can fix

I honestly don't know
If every piece will be tied up
But with each additional knot
I am brought closer
To a fuller understanding of God

#BecauseOfRHE
written: May 8th

Because of RHE
It seems impossible to communicate
What this stranger meant to me
Woman of valor
Eshet Chayil
Her words helped me heal

Because of RHE
I understand in deeper ways
Theology
Resiliency
Dignity

Because of RHE
I have my first tattoo
Etched into my skin
To serve as a reminder
Of who God says I am
And who I strive to be
Alongside other valorous women
(Hey Danielle and Kari!)

Because of RHE
I feel more fully, truly free
To evolve
To love
God
Myself
And others
Better

Woman Wisdom Calling
written: May 8th

Would people even know
Wisdom was calling them
Personified as a woman

Would people even know
Wisdom was calling them
Personified as a woman

Women Walking with Jesus
written: May 17th

I heard someone
Somewhere say
Jesus didn't have to ask
The women to follow him
They just did

What Do "Biblical" Men and Women Look Like
written: May 20th

When Pastor Derwin was preaching a sermon
He referenced the "fruit of the Spirit"
As the answer to the question
Of what "biblical" men and women look like

He did not connect biblical womanhood
To being a mother or wife
This was a word for women
In all circumstances of life
To cultivate
Love, joy, peace, patience,
Kindness, goodness, faithfulness,
Gentleness, and self-control

Moving past the false gender binary
Here's the thing
When *people* are rooted in love
Growing
Bearing fruit
We are producing the same sweet products

The fight over gender roles is old
Decades
Centuries
Millennia
Ago and ago and ago
From the earliest iteration of "the curse"

Cultural influence
Influencing culture
Losing influence
Grasping
Forcing
Doubling down on stereotypes
When generalizations
Preferences and
Skewed interpretations
Are all many have to go on

It is a waste of time
Trying to change people
Into someone they are not
When focusing on putting people in a box
Our time would be better spent
Encouraging the "fruit of the Spirit"
In one another
In love, joy, peace, patience,
Kindness, goodness, faithfulness,
Gentleness, and self-control

To All the Christian Men I Knew Before
written: May 20th

I am no longer satisfied
With being vilified
Or vilifying my neighbor
Objectification
Results in the defamation
Of the image I bear
Of the one you call Savior

Stop prioritizing
The comfort of men
So you can value me as a human
Call out sexism
In yourself and others

If you aren't doing the work
Of healing from patriarchy
And everything it's connected to
Then, you aren't being a friend
Because you've shown
You can't be bothered by
Issues that are important to me
That affect me physically,
Emotionally, mentally, and spiritually
That impact my well-being

Work with me toward the day
When we no longer say
"Women are equal to"
As if men are the standard
And work with me toward the day
When the existence is celebrated
Of people outside the false gender binary

If you love me
Labor until all people
Know our worth
Apart from the attention
Or affirmation of cishet men

Were They Ever Made Like This?
written: June 22nd

For a good four years or more
I just couldn't get myself
Out of bed in the mornings
Especially during the week
When my one adult interactee had to leave
But Stephen was so patient with me
Never once requiring more of me
Joyfully and sacrificially
Picking up all the slack
Always respecting when I had no energy
Without making me feel guilty
Because as a human being
I am to be valued for more than my body

I've heard things like
"They just don't make 'em like they used to"
But I'm not sure the elusive "they" ever did
A world run by patriarchy
Historically and currently
Leaves no space for men like this
I realize I am #blessed
As I read a text Ms. Donna sent
"He's one of the good ones"

But it is past time
For Stephen to be an anomaly
And TBH the bar is set
Unbelievably low for him
Compared to the scrutiny
I've experienced

Stephen could teach classes
If that would help
But I just don't know if it would
So, "man manufacturer"
If you read these words
Could you make more of 'em
Like Stephen?

Nicki Pappas

My Life Like a Lived in House
written: May 16th

Our house is so v "lived in"
With smudges
Stains
And stripped away paint
Whenever we have company
Especially if I'm hosting a party
I have the urge to conceal
All that is unsightly
This endeavor is practically impossible
And definitely unfruitful
And oh, how this tendency
Rears its head in me
As I seek to mask my imperfections
Defend against false perceptions
And ignore severe self-deception
In all its forms

To protect myself
I guard information
Careful to not be too vulnerable
But when I'm nervous
Or prematurely comfortable
I break my own rule
And disclose too much
I fear if people know
The trauma and pain of my past
They will view me differently
Pull away from me
Or simply try to "fix" me
Without an ounce of empathy

The hard part is that
These very fears have come to pass
On more occasions than I can count
People I trusted and counted on
Gone when the going got tough
I get it and don't hold anything against them
These are just observations

Not condemnations
I am learning that freedom and flourishing
Are ushered in
When I stop hiding my fears and failures
Because my people will love and accept me anyway

With wisdom and discernment
Boundaries drawn for my soul and
People who want me to be whole
Healing is on the horizon and it's already here

A Poem to My Kids
written: June 23rd

Oh, what lovely beings you are
Each of you a shining star
Always remember the joy you bring
Smiles that are contagious
Even when your behavior is outrageous
You're worth me sacrificing so many things

If You Live Like Jesus
written: May 23rd

A telling indication of humility
And the character of Jesus being reflected
Is the type of people who surround you
And the type of people who despise you

WWJD
written: June 1st

I talk of how Jesus flipped tables
To justify my anger
Toward grievances when offended
And claim I'm able to administer
This same treatment
Often using this tactic on those
With whom I disagree
Even on minor things

I can't possibly know
All the factors that influenced
The decision to table flip
While appearing to flip a switch
Looking like flipping out to those around
And flipping the standards

I do know it was those in the temple
On the receiving end
The only times recorded
Where an exchange like this occurred
Though there were other interactions
In which the prideful
Reaped the reward for their hubris
In the form of harsh verbal rebukes

I need to slow down
When I want to drag
The hypocritical people I know
Through the mud
Because when Nicodemus humbly visited Jesus
He was met with compassion and kindness

Pause
Take a deep breath
The next time I see tables
That I should or shouldn't try
To overturn in the name of Christ
Before I do something Jesus would or wouldn't do

I need to remember
To first remove the log
Obstructing my view
While focusing on loving others
In word and deed
And scanning my surroundings
For signs of curiosity

Hope in Doubt
written: Aug. 13, 2018

Even in the midst of
Immense pain and sorrow
I have hope for today
And (sometimes) for tomorrow
This does not mean
I am without any doubt
But I am trusting
In the times of drought
That refreshment will come
This doesn't hinge on me
Not coming undone
I can argue and wrestle
Like Job, Jacob, and RHE
Commemorating divine interactions
With Hagar's *El Roi* who sees
I vow to love
I vow to press on
I vow to hope as I'm able
Day by day by day

[Note: I wrote about hope in doubt before I really *felt* hopeful. That's why this poem was placed near the end of the timeline even though it was written in August 2018.]

I Can't Call It Quits
written: June 6th

In spite of it all
I can't call it quits
On what I learned to call "the Church"

I think everyone has to come
Out of disillusionment
At their own pace
It took intentional internal examination
For me to come face to face
With the ways I allowed spiritual abuse
To run rampant in my life
Increasing over the years in intensity
More always demanded of me
Little support or encouragement along the way
Shame upon shame upon shame piled on top
Suffocating
Self-inflicted spiritual suffering
"For Jesus"
Being part of a death
(Rather than resurrection and life)
Focused people
But unwavering loyalty expected nevertheless

Sitting down twice
With the one
Who holds all the power
My character maligned
Having nefarious motives assigned
Harsh accusations leveled against me
As if I would thrive off of pointing out
Potential pitfalls that aren't on your radar
Simply desiring to help you identify faulty beliefs
Because I am thankful for those who helped me
I didn't think you were a bad guy
Certainly not worse than others
And I gave the very best of myself for years
Just to show how much love
I had for you

Your family
And each member of the Body
None of it mattered in the end
My voice effectively silenced
I was put in my place
I knew I could not bring up your failures
Unless I was prepared to receive your wrath again
But unwavering loyalty expected nevertheless

Leaving a willfully dysfunctional local church
Does not mean forsaking the gospel
Breaking free from toxicity
Sharing my story in the hopes
That there would be some accountability
Alas, I am the one experiencing scrutiny
As people who know both full and partial details
Speculate and spout off that we
Needed to give the situation more time
They know we were irreparably damaged
Yet some drive the dagger even further in my heart
To not even have my private text message responded to
While public tributes are dedicated to
Those who left on better terms
The hot, stinging tears I blink back
Because I am ashamed at the thought
Of shedding a single tear on those
Who haven't cried for me
I am shocked by the members that know
Each time I walked through the doors
I was gripped by fear
But unwavering loyalty expected nevertheless

I do not breeze past the victories, though
No matter how seemingly small
Of the brave people who pressed in
In the past and present
In the way that was best for them
For some that meant
Trying another church
Speaking truth to power
No matter how much it hurts
Recording podcasts and publishing books

Traveling to talk with gathered misfits
Trying to spark better ways
Of thinking about God, ourselves, and others
Acts upon acts upon acts of resistance and holy rebellion
Letting evil know it will not win
The examples I have to follow
I won't let their relentless labor be wasted
Unwavering loyalty to myself and the healing of humanity

In spite of it all
I can't call it quits
On what I learned to call "the Church"

[Note: From Sept. 2019 until January 2021, I didn't attend church. During that time, some may think I did call it quits on what I learned to call "the Church." I'll leave that up to you.]

Part E.
Conclusion

Rediscovering Myself

I once thought I was fatally flawed
With no hope but Christ
Though others already knew I wasn't perfect
I didn't think twice
About wearing a mask and concealing
The truth of who I am
My Enneagram personality type
Is referred to as a chameleon
Because to be deemed worthless
And seen as a failure
Is my biggest fear

As I've been learning about myself
I'm shedding tears
Because I finally feel known
And believe I'm not alone
I am slowly
Very slowly
Finding my way home

Discovering New Depths of God

I may no longer identify as evangelical
But I still take Christianity seriously
I repeatedly worked through
Genesis one through four
Studied new words
Identified repetition
Learned more about the cultural context
And had preconceived notions challenged

Theology matters
What we believe about God
Impacts how we view God, ourselves, and others
If I don't grasp the foundation set in the first chapters
I can't grasp the rest of the biblical texts
Or I can pridefully think I do
And this presents problems, too

One of the most dangerous experiences for me
Is thinking I fully understand something
I love theology
And I love learning
Unfortunately, most of my synthesizing
Was done in an echo chamber
Now, I am seeking out people
Who push me to wrestle with God
I have never felt more scared or more secure

In my finite comprehension
I could be wrong about it all
No matter where I land
(Or if I land at all - S/O to Marla)
It's so arrogant of me to think
I ever had the infinite all figured out
This season has been wrought with doubt
But the world will keep turning
Apart from my certitude
I don't need to resolve
One single uncertainty

It is simultaneously terrifying and liberating
To lay down my pride
Of always having to be right
Or enforce my interpretation
Bring your hesitancies
Inhibitions
Cynicism
And apprehension
If you need to talk
I'm here with a listening ear
I'll hear you
Without trying to "fix" you
Or sway you my way

I am eternally grateful
For the people who haven't ostracized me
In my striving and struggling
Who have been a steady representation
Of God not forsaking me
Thank you for being the most approachable people

Acknowledgements

I want to thank all of my newfound guides.
Without you, I literally wouldn't be here.

Thank you for reading
Reflections from a Former Evangelical:
Poems Reminiscent of My 2019 Worldview.
If you enjoyed this book, please share an
online review on Amazon and Goodreads.

KEEP IN TOUCH WITH NICKI PAPPAS

Website: nickipappas.com
Podcast: *Broadening the Narrative*
Instagram: @broadeningthenarrative
TikTok: @broadeningthenarrative
Twitter: @broadnarrative
Facebook: facebook.com/groups/
broadeningthenarrative